The Shadow of
the Hummingbird

The Shadow of
the Hummingbird

Athol Fugard

*With a Prelude by Paula Fourie,
with extracts from Athol Fugard's
unpublished notebooks*

THEATRE COMMUNICATIONS GROUP
NEW YORK
2014

The Shadow of the Hummingbird is published by Theatre Communications Group, Inc., 520 8th Avenue, 24th Floor, New York, NY 10018-4156

The publication of *The Shadow of the Hummingbird*, by Athol Fugard, through TCG's Book Program, is made possible in part by the New York State Council on the Arts with the support of Governor Andrew Cuomo and the New York State Legislature.

TCG books are exclusively distributed to the book trade by Consortium Book Sales and Distribution.

LIBRARY OF CONGRESS CATALOGING-IN-PUBLICATION DATA
Fugard, Athol.
The shadow of the hummingbird / by Athol Fugard ; with an introductory prelude by Paula Fourie, with extracts from Athol Fugard's unpublished notebooks.
pages cm
ISBN 978-1-55936-482-9 (trade paper)
ISBN 978-1-55936-795-0 (ebook)
I. Title.
PR9369.3.F8S47   2014
822—dc23   2014006774

Book design and composition by Lisa Govan
Cover design by Lisa Govan
Front and back cover photos © Ann Johansson/Corbis

First Edition, March 2014

For Gavyn

Contents

Acknowledgments

The authors would like to thank The Lilly Library at Indiana University in Bloomington for facilitating access to Mr. Fugard's unpublished notebooks.

Production History

The Shadow of the Hummingbird received its world premiere at the Long Wharf Theatre (Gordon Edelstein, Artistic Director; Joshua Borenstein, Managing Director) in New Haven, Connecticut, on April 2, 2014. The production was directed by Gordon Edelstein. The scenic design was by Eugene Lee, the costume design was by Susan Hilferty, the lighting design was by Michael Chybowski, the sound design was by John Gromada and the production stage manager was Jason Kaiser. The cast was:

OUPA   Athol Fugard
BOBA   Aiden McMillan/
                                             Dermot McMillan

Characters

OUPA: an ailing old man in his eighties
BOBA: his grandson, ten years old

The Shadow of
the Hummingbird

———

He lives a day.
What is he? What is he not?
Man is a dream of a shadow.

—Pindar, Pythian 8, 95–6

Prelude

A small room with an old armchair facing one of the walls. There is a large square of sunlight on the wall from the room's one window. There is also a door and a couple of over-loaded bookcases against the other walls. On one side of the room is a crowded desk with odds and ends, piles of books and a glass of water. Beside the armchair is a small side table with a few books. A reading lamp of sorts, fountain pens and pencils. It is the room of someone who reads. Hidden somewhere in the clutter, a pair of large wire spectacles.

An old man, Oupa, wearing a dressing gown over striped flannel pajamas, comes shuffling onto the stage, muttering under his breath:

OUPA: Spectacles . . . spectacles . . . where are my bloody eyes?

(Surveying the cluttered room.)

What a spectacle!

(Shaking his head ruefully, he moves around the room, searching until he finds his spectacles.)

Ah!

(He puts them on, opening his eyes wide.)

Spectacular spectacles! *(Takes them off and polishes them)* A contraption devised to grant, once more, the gift of sight to the decrepit, those of us whose faculties have been eroded by time, nerve endings ground down to little stumps. We who move slowly now. But do they help you *see*? The old and infirm haven't lost their sight, they have merely turned their gaze inward.

(Meditatively:)

As I once heard a wise sage say, "Young man, the final landscape is within."

(Turning to face the wall with the square of sunlight, he stares at it for a few moments. Then he abruptly heads for a bookcase, muttering urgently:)

Shadow, shadow . . . shadow!

(There is a barely contained excitement in his body now, an energy in his movements, even though they are stiff and slow. He has a purpose: he is searching for something. He scans the books on one of the shelves, mumbling under his breath, then pulls one out. It is one of his own notebooks, all of which look different [some spiral bound, some hardcover], but are all filled with handwritten notes. He pages quickly through the notebook before slowing down and finally stopping. Adjusting his spec-

tacles, he brings the notebook closer to his face, reading aloud, tasting the words on his tongue, relishing them:)

Bird sightings, Summer 1997/1998, Port Elizabeth:

> Forest Weaver
> Lesser-collared Sunbird
> Red-eyed Dove
> Olive Thrush
> Paradise Flycatcher
> Gray-headed Sparrow
> Cape White-eye
> Sombre Bulbul
> Laughing Dove
> Cattle Egret
> Streaky-headed Seedeater
> Spectacled Weaver *(Laughing at the reference to spectacles)*
> Fork-tailed Drongo
> Cape Wagtail
> Terrestrial Bulbul
> Swee Waxbill
> Speckled Mousebird
> Tambourine Dove
> Black-headed Heron
> Cinnamon Dove
> Bar-throated Apalis
> Glossy Starling
> Black Sunbird
> Fiscal Flycatcher
> Brown-hooded Kingfisher
> Pearl-breasted Swallow
> Knysna Loerie
> Helmeted Guinea Fowl
> Bou-bou Shrike

(Triumphantly:)

Dikkop!

(Chuckling quietly as he turns the word around in his head, repeating it under his breath:)

Dikkop . . . Dikkop . . . In English, the Cape Thick-knee, in Afrikaans . . .

(A pause. Laughing.)

Dikkop . . . Thick-head!

(Still laughing, adopting a pedantic tone as he reads:)

The *Dikkop* is found in Southern Africa. A solitary bird by nature, it nests in small scrapes in the hot dry earth. The *Dikkop* will perform melodramatic "injury displays" to lure any predator away from its nest.

(Pausing to think. Then he reads:)

These birds are quiet during the day but, at night, their mournful whistles can be heard over long distances . . .

(Looking down, examining his pajamas and worn slippers.)

Ah! So that's what I am! The lesser blue-and-white-striped Thick-head. An old bird, and of a bald variety. Spectacularly spectacled, too!

(Laughing, he picks up the edges of his dressing gown and flaps his arms feebly.)

Dikkop! I am a Thick-head!

(Still laughing, he continues paging through the note-book until he reaches the following entry, which he reads aloud:)

September 21, 1997

Sat out on the balcony this morning and almost swooned under the caress of a warm sun in a clear sky. With a gentle breeze fluttering over my body . . . memories of the dreamy sensual haze I used to surrender to on the rocks after a dive. How I love discovering and feeling the memories stored up in my body, memories that half the time my tired old mind can't place and locate.

(Smiling gently at the memory, he turns a few pages back to an earlier entry. He reads aloud:)

August 13

Living through another Death and once again I know that it is only through love that I will resurrect myself. I am truly dead and dark inside; I must open all my doors and windows and let in the light. This morning's epiphany: a visit from a Crested Barbet with a fledgling . . . the adult bird fed the young one on pawpaw.

(A hint of a frown has appeared on his forehead. His eyes travel to the bottom of the page and he reads aloud:)

Another appalling night—lurid and repulsive dreams. I'm a terrible mess inside.

(The frown on his forehead has deepened. He discards the notebook. Turning to the bookcase once more, he

pulls out a second notebook. He glances at the first entry, then places it back randomly in the bookcase. He pulls out a third notebook, glances at the first page, then pages through it quickly.)

1974 . . . 1974 . . .

(Shaking his head, he returns the notebook to a shelf. Pausing, he stands in front of the bookcase for a few seconds, as if accessing a mental index of it. He shrugs. It is clear that he has no idea where the notebook that he is looking for is. His eyes scan the shelves from a distance, then, when his eyes catch the lowest shelf, he goes down abruptly on his knees, holding onto the bookcase as he lowers himself. On all fours now, he pulls out six notebooks from the shelf. Clutching them to his chest with one hand, he tries to get up. Just as he seems to be succeeding, the notebooks slip from his hand and fall to the floor.)

Damnit!

(A spell of coughing, as he holds his hand to his chest. He lowers himself again and gently gathers the notebooks. This time, he manages to get to the armchair safely, and settles down with the notebooks. He is visibly tired and closes his eyes for a few seconds, breathing heavily. Now, seemingly recovered, he opens the first notebook and begins to page hurriedly through it. He suddenly stops, reads silently for a moment, then begins to laugh. He pages on, only to return to this particular entry to read it again, then laughs once more. He places the notebook on the floor. He opens the second notebook and pages through it until he stops at the following entry, which he reads aloud:)

December 1988

All of me is now finally back home in Port Elizabeth and in tune with the simple but powerful rhythms of this scrubby coastline. What makes me conscious of this is the way I can again appreciate, just sit and watch the big winds of this world . . . and once again they move me as deeply as they ever did. Rivers of wind—long and unending—they flow through the house, through my life, with the same spiritual potency that the great Ganges has for an Indian soul. And because it's high summer now, and a powerful sun blazes out of an intense blue sky almost every day, the winds are full of light . . . rivers of light! With the trees splashing around in them.

(He continues paging for a short while, then places the notebook on the floor, muttering impatiently:)

Sentimental bloody idiot. Shadows, shadows . . . shadows!

(He opens a thrid notebook and glances at the first page:)

2012!

(Visibly distressed, he rises from his chair to return the notebook to the bookcase. Then, changing his mind, he opens the notebook. He reads aloud:)

You loved my body the way van Gogh loved those old boots which so inspire me. In painting them, van Gogh was loving them as symbols of all of toiling, suffering and, finally, dying Humanity. What he really painted with that canvass was the soul of all mankind that an undeserving God claims as his, asserting the right to judge the value and virtue of that tired, sweat-stained leather. But—and it's a big but, my beloved—if van Gogh himself needed a new pair of boots for all his tramping around, would he go out looking for a pair like the ones he painted? So, I ask you, my beloved, "Isn't that the way you love my body? But, with all your years still ahead of you, is it what you need?"

(Turning the page, he reads aloud:)

A scribbled riddle:

> How do you know when something is finished
> And time to throw it away?
> Like all holy things
> Old shoes and boots will answer:
> "Walk one more mile in me."

(Still disturbed, he continues paging through the note-book. He has forgotten the urgency of his search. He reaches a later entry, which he reads aloud:)

A butterfly has just flown through a small cloud of my pipe smoke . . . and did not cough.

(He laughs gently, then continues to read:)

It has now settled on a grapevine.

(He moves to the bottom of the same page:)

Determined to bring my pipe-smoking under control. Seriously concerned about my physical weakness. Old age or too much stress.

(The old man closes the notebook and looks furtively around him, then digs deep into the pocket of his dressing gown and retrieves his pipe. He strokes it lovingly, then puts it in his mouth. What follows is an elaborate display of pretending to stop his pipe with tobacco, tamping it down firmly, then lighting it. He sits back and puffs himself up with imaginary smoke. Closing his eyes, he breathes out. Speaking in a dramatic voice:)

Ah, the thick creamy satisfaction of my Kapp and Peterson filled with rum-and-maple tobacco.

(He takes another drag, then breathes out, all the while enjoying the sensation of the "smoke" rising and wafting around his head. Taking another drag from his pipe:)

I am infused . . .

(He blows out the "smoke" with a ferocious face. Leaning forward with hands outstretched, he is ready to pounce.)

. . . with dragon's courage!

(He coughs. Lowering his voice, chuckling feebly:)

Though I'm the only one who can see it now.

(For the rest of the time in his chair, he continues "smoking" his pipe, sometimes letting it rest in his mouth, at other times holding it in his hand. He opens the fourth notebook in his lap. He pages leisurely through it until he stops near the middle and reads aloud:)

September . . .

(Turning quickly to the first page:)

. . . 1983

(Turning back to the original entry:)

From the other side of the back door to the shed an exquisitely mysterious little song, like clear water playing with pebbles . . . the two Stripe-breasted Swallows have returned to their nest above the door. What can I say? The agonies I have suffered in past seasons, watching them trying to build that nest—they have never and never will get the entrance tunnel right because of the corrugations in the aluminum roof—and now there they are again and no doubt will waste no time in trying once more. Another season of despair? I was thinking about this as I stood listening to the breathtaking small secrecy of their rippling chatter, when in a flash I realized that, "No, it would not be another essay in hopelessness." As beautiful as it would have been to have a perfect nest up there, to have had a "happy ending," their return to the broken one is an even profounder metaphor of something I must now meditate on and try to understand.

(He continues paging through the notebook, stopping occasionally to read silently to himself. He reaches the following entry, which he reads aloud:)

A lot of emotional tension inside me tonight . . . the work that lies ahead at this desk, the desperate need for rain, the good-bye to this world at the end of February, then New York.

(A pause as his eyes travel across the page, reading one or two sentences silently. Then he reads aloud:)

So much to love and look after! The last addiction in my life will be loving—the ecstasy of possession, the exquisite pain of loss. I know that I will have to give that up—the gross, material aspect of it—even as I have had to give up drinking. If I live long enough my inner self will demand it as surely as it demanded my present sobriety.

(He pages to the end of the notebook, where he reads aloud:)

Tonight I was surprised to discover with what eagerness I am waiting for a grandchild.

(He gets up, digs in his pocket, and retrieves a wristwatch with a broken strap. After glancing at it impatiently, he approaches the window, peering through it into the distance. He is searching for something or someone. Then he resumes his reading:)

I always knew I was looking forward to one but never quite realized the extent of my impatience. I found myself positively squirming with anticipated pleasure as I thought about the things I would like to do with him or her. I think there is a good chance of me being the most doting grandfather any child ever had! It's the sharing of life that I want to get into.

(He is clearly delighted at having found this entry. Turning a few pages back, he tries to date it:)

January 1984!

(Returning to his chair, he discards the notebook, then stares pointedly at the sunlit wall once more. Nothing

happens. He opens the fifth notebook to a random page, scans it briefly, and reads aloud:)

November 28, 1993

When my mind is finally useless, I'll try just running and walking through the world and letting my body remember the wonderful life it has lived, as it did today as I ran through dappled sunlight, the scents of the earth, and bird song.

(He closes the notebook.)

(Laughing) Running when your mind is finally useless! Ha! Good luck to you, young man!

(Tossing the notebook on the floor, he picks up the sixth one. Glancing at the first page:)

1981.

(Opening the notebook on a random page, he reads aloud:)

No hope. My fingernails will always be dirty.

(Glancing at his nails, shaking his head incredulously, and laughing.)

Still no hope!

(He continues to page, then stops abruptly and reads aloud:)

A final few moments each night when I put off the last light in the lounge and pace the room in the dark, myself and the books on the shelves having lost the power of speech.

(A thoughtful pause. Then he continues to read aloud:)

Just about every night now, I dream about birds.

(He turns a few pages backward, scanning, searching. Then he reads aloud:)

Beginning to see the light at the end of the tunnel. One of these days I'll have a shadow again.

(He closes the book quickly, placing it on the floor next to the other notebooks. He has remembered his search and his earlier haste. He puts down his pipe on the side table. Muttering feverishly, gesturing with one hand.)

Shadow, shadow . . . shadow!

(Visibly agitated now, he rises heavily and approaches the bookcase once more. In quick succession, he pulls out two notebooks, pages hurriedly through them and puts them back randomly. He pulls out a third notebook, perhaps from a different shelf.)

It's got to be this one.

(Paging through the notebook with a quiet focus, first rapidly then slowing down, he stops. He has found the entry that he has been searching for all along and reads aloud, with excitement and reverence:)

December 1963

The end of the year. Nothing could mean less to me. I will lie in bed tonight and, as I have done so many nights, watch the shadow of a tree on our stoep through our opened doors. The curtains will breathe gently, with a soft wind, and the shadow itself will move, clotting into blackness on the cool stone or breaking apart into the agitated contours of leaves; and, as on so many nights now, I will fall asleep in the unimportant labyrinth of a dialogue that I follow through as if learnt by rote. First my mind consciously analyzes the phenomenon of a shadow, the fall of light, etc., and assures me that a shadow is nothing. Then with my eyes, with all the sense of my living mortal body, I look at "it"—"it"—and savor the beauty of its being. Yet it is nothing. My mind has told me so, and proved it. And my wonder increases, encompassing now not only the beauty of the shadow but the duplicity, the paradox that runs so richly through all this life. And then sleep.

(He pauses for a moment. Then, suddenly beaming with pride, he gives the notebook a kiss and places it carefully on his side table.)

The play follows seamlessly after the Prelude.

Oupa shuffles toward the wall with the square of sun-light. As he approaches it, his shadow creeps slowly up from the floor. He holds out his arms in a welcoming embrace.

OUPA: Me . . . my dark shape . . . my very own unique little patch of darkness.

(He amuses himself for a few seconds by playing feebly with his shadow. He applauds his efforts with a weak little chuckle.)

In Afrikaans . . . my skaduwee . . . In Spanish . . . mi sombra . . . French . . . mon ombre . . . German . . . mein Schatten . . . my ever faithful companion . . . my shadow . . .

(Singing as he attempts a feeble dance:)

Like the wallpaper sticks to the wall
Like the seashore clings to the sea

Like you'll never get rid of your shadow
Frank, you'll never get rid of me.

Let all the others fight and fuss
Whatever happens, we've got us.

Me and my shadow
We're closer than pages that stick in a book . . .

*(Adopting the tone and pedantic attitude of the teacher
he was once:)*

Shadow. The word can of course also be used figuratively
to suggest an atmosphere of ominous oppressiveness . . .
or also sadness and gloom. As for example:

A shadow of gloom and mourning fell over the
nations with the news of his death.

The usage I prefer to dwell on today, though, is when it
refers to an inferior remnant or version of something such
as . . .

(He tries to straighten up.)

This once fine figure of a man . . .

(He sinks back into his now customary stooping posture.)

. . . has become a shadow of his former self.

(His shadow follows him in more contortions.
   *Boba appears in the doorway. He is burdened with a
school backpack. He stands watching the old man silently
for a few seconds.)*

20

BOBA: Oupa . . . Oupa! . . .

(Twisting his body as best he can, the old man turns on Boba with a ferocious roar.)

What are you doing?

OUPA: What's the matter with you, Boba . . . are you blind? I've transmogrified!

BOBA: Into what?

OUPA: The teacher from the black lagoon! And I am hungry for your tender white meat . . . so defend yourself.

BOBA: He doesn't frighten me anymore, Oupa. And, anyway, we've stopped playing with wooden swords . . . haven't we?

OUPA: For God's sake, Boba! . . . Have you forgotten everything I've taught you? Unsheathe the sword of your imagination, boy, because here I come!

(Slipping off his school backpack and using it as a shield and unsheathing the imaginary sword of his imagination, Boba eludes a charge from the monster. A terrible fight ensues in the course of which Boba delivers one mortal blow after another. The teacher from the black lagoon keeps wanting to end the fight and die but Boba doesn't let him, with a: "Not yet. I'm not finished." He does eventually kill the totally exhausted creature who falls to the ground with a terrible cry and lies there twitching as his life ebbs away.)

Come now . . . finish me off . . . you know the routine.

(Boba puts his foot on Oupa's chest and, holding his sword with both hands, he delivers the mortal thrust.)

BOBA: Die! . . . You worm-faced creature of the night!

OUPA *(Crawling to his chair with a groan)*: Merciful Heaven. Why did it take you so long? Was your sword blunt? I thought it was never going to end.

BOBA: Your skin was very thick, Oupa.

OUPA *(Hands to his heart)*: Ooooh! That my lord was a deadlier thrust than any of those your Excalibur inflicted. But, pray tell me, at whose hand did I have the honor, the agony, and the ecstasy of dying this time?

BOBA: Prince Gruffydd of Deheubarth.

OUPA *(Suddenly an old, cringing menial)*: Ay . . . ay . . . and a nobler lord never defended the sacred soil of Wales.

But come now, my master . . . let us now put aside our weapons and turn our minds to more mundane matters . . . How are things at home?

BOBA: Same as usual.

OUPA: Which I take it means you are in the dog-box again. What did it this time?

BOBA: Didn't do my homework.

OUPA: As you well know, my cherished one, I hate to say anything in support of your father, but he might be right this time . . . And now to top it all, they, of course, don't know where you are.

BOBA: No.

OUPA: So where are you supposed to be?

BOBA: At Norell's house doing homework.

OUPA *(Groaning)*: Oh God, Boba . . . what are we going to do?

BOBA: About what, Oupa?

OUPA: Me and you. Sooner or later they are going to find out that you are secretly visiting me again. And then you will be in very hot water with your dad.

BOBA: If you just say you are sorry, Oupa.

(Oupa starts to shake his head, protesting.)

And that you won't call him a stupid ox again, he will allow me . . .

OUPA *(Flaring up)*: No! I'll drop the ox but not the qualifying adjective . . . because that is what he is and I know your mother secretly agrees with me. I know he is my son, but, believe me, Boba, that, as God's dirty tricks go, giving him to me as my one and only heir, is by far the dirtiest one he has ever played on me. When he first married your mother, and she became pregnant, I lived in mortal terror of the possibility that another idiot was on the way. All I can say is thank God for your mother. She must have provided the genes that are responsible for you. And just for the record, he is the one that should apologize to me for his impertinence in trying to tell me . . . me! . . . that . . . I am . . . what did he say I was?

BOBA: An arrogant and conceited old idiot.

OUPA: Please, Boba, don't say it with such relish. Arrogant and conceited! And all because I corrected him in pointing out that anyone claiming to being well-educated would know that it was the Sumerians in three thousand B.C. who launched literacy on the world. But that was just a smoke screen to hide the real issue. The struggle for your beautiful young mind. Conformity or rebellion. Oh yes! What was the first lesson I taught you, Boba?

BOBA: The one you made me write out ten times?

OUPA: Yes.

BOBA: If I don't understand something . . . ask a question.

OUPA *(Delighted)*: Yes. If you have any doubts about the so-called wisdom of this age . . . question it, boy! That's all that a wise old Greek called Socrates tried to teach his young friends . . . but the result? The charge of corrupting the youth. The verdict . . . guilty! The penalty . . . a cup of hemlock . . . poison.

BOBA *(Interrupting his grandfather, urgently, pointing at the wall)*: Oupa! . . . Oupa! . . . Look! There it is.

(A blurred little smudge of a shadow is hovering and flitting around in the square of sunlight on the wall. The old man is immediately silenced. He and the boy fall back to the armchair where the old man sits and the boy kneels beside him. They watch the shadow for a good few minutes before it suddenly streaks across the patch of sunlight and is gone . . .

The boy then jumps up and darts across to the window and looks outside.)

Gone!

OUPA: Is the feeder full?

BOBA: Yes.

(After one more look through the window in all directions, Boba rejoins his grandfather.)

OUPA: He'll be back.

(He realizes the boy is staring at him.)

What now?

BOBA: You know, Oupa . . . if we just pull your chair over here, you can sit and watch the real bird and not just its shadow.

OUPA: Oh for God's sake, Boba! So that's your opinion of me, is it? An idiot like your father?

BOBA: Don't you want to see the real bird, Oupa?

OUPA: Boba, I've spent enough time watching real hummingbirds—and in this case it happens to be Anna's Hummingbird—to last me for the rest of my life. But that's not the point. It's that shadow on the wall . . . the central image in Plato's *Republic*. In his case, of course, it wasn't an untidy little room where an old man is waiting for what has become the monumentally boring end to his life, but a cave in which all the people sit chained watching shadows on the wall . . .

(Opening a book from his side table.)

Here's how Plato described it:

> Imagine men who live in an underground cave, which emerges into the outer light that seeps into the cave's depths. From childhood, these men have their legs and necks chained in such a way that they are forced to remain in one spot and can only see what is in front of them. Behind them, higher up, and a slight distance away, imagine a fire burning; between the prisoners and the fire is a road with a low wall running beside it, like a screen over which puppeteers perform their shows.

(He looks at Boba.)

Just as I thought. You don't understand a word, do you?

BOBA: No, I don't. Sorry, Oupa.

OUPA: You are forgiven. I'll try again . . . and slowly . . . but listen carefully!

(He is now in his element. He gets to his feet and goes to the wall.)

Imagine this is the wall of a cave. It is a big cave and you are one of a countless number of people who are sitting like you staring at this wall. You've been chained to your seat so you can only stare at the wall in front of you. What you can't see is that behind you there is a big blazing fire which casts light on this wall. There are no windows. Now imagine a little hummingbird flies into the cave and starts flitting around behind your back, between you and the fire. What will you see on the wall? No! . . . I can already see stupidity in the making. Give yourself time. Think! You, the hummingbird, the fire. What do you see on that wall?

(Pause.)

BOBA: The shadow of the hummingbird.
OUPA: Precisely!

(He is ecstatically happy.)

There is still hope for you, my boy! But let us proceed! What we have to imagine now is that, because they are in chains, they have spent their whole lives watching shadows on the wall. What does that mean?
BOBA: I don't know, Oupa.
OUPA: Yes, you do, but you've forgotten *that you know*. I remember very clearly a moment in your infancy—you weren't even a toddler yet—your mother and I were having a cup of afternoon tea and she had put you down on the floor so that you could crawl around. I remember that moment because that is when you gave me my first lesson in Plato's theory of forms. You see, I noticed that instead of crawling around, you were getting very frustrated because you couldn't pick up a little shadow you had found on the floor—it was the shadow of a lovely red rose I had given your mother. It was in a vase on the windowsill. I know you can't remember that, but the

question is: Why on earth did you want to pick up a little shadow you had found on the floor?

BOBA: Because . . .

OUPA: Yes. Go on. Be brave . . . say it.

BOBA: . . . because I . . . I wanted to play with it?

OUPA: Exactly! You thought it was a real thing that you could bite and smell and taste the way babies do with things. Not so?

BOBA: Yes.

OUPA: And those people sitting there in the cave who have never been able to leave it because they are chained to their places, what do they think about that shadow flitting around on the wall?

BOBA: They also think it is real.

OUPA: Well done. Now comes the exciting part, Boba. Imagine that one of them somehow manages to free himself from his chains.

BOBA: How, Oupa?

OUPA: Oh for Heaven's sake, Boba . . . anyhow you like . . . the important thing is he is free. So now what does he do? Come on. Imagine it was you. What would you do?

BOBA: Get out of the cave as fast as I could.

OUPA: Right! You turn around and make a dash for it. But what happens then?

BOBA: I escape. I am free.

OUPA: Not so fast. Remember you have been living in darkness all your life.

BOBA: So?

OUPA: What do you mean, "so"?

(Impatiently:)

Think, boy! Think! What happens to you when you step out of a dark room into bright light?

BOBA: I have to blink. I can't see very well.

OUPA: Exactly. You stumble around for a bit but, gradually, gradually your eyes get used to the light, and then one day you look up and what do you really see for the first time in all its shimmering glory?

BOBA: The hummingbird?

OUPA *(Triumphantly applauding the boy's answer)*: Exactly!!! Bravo, bravo! Well done, Boba, well done!

(He waits for a matching response from Boba. Boba stares back at him blankly.)

BOBA: Go on.

OUPA: What do you mean, "go on"? There's no going on. That is it.

BOBA: That's all?

OUPA *(Outraged)*: Your response to Plato's allegory is a dismissive: "That's all?"

BOBA: Sorry, Oupa, but it's just . . . well, Mr. Plato's story is not a very good one, Oupa.

OUPA: So what do you want. Must he get his gun, shoot the bloody bird and then eat it?

BOBA *(Apologetically)*: I'm sorry, Oupa.

OUPA: I give up!

(The old man throws up his hands in disgust and fumes away in silence.)

BOBA *(Trying to break a very strained silence)*: Do you want to help me with my homework, Oupa?

OUPA: I'm not a teacher anymore. Go ask the idiot who's teaching you right now.

BOBA: So . . . Would you like me to go, Oupa?

(No response from the old man. Boba collects his back-pack.)

I'll go now.

(He starts to leave.)

OUPA: No! Come back.

(Boba puts down his backpack and waits.)

My turn to say sorry.
BOBA: You didn't do anything wrong, Oupa . . . except . . .

(Pause.)

OUPA: Except what?
BOBA: . . . except get a little bit cross with me.
OUPA *(Bridling yet another insult)*: A little bit cross? I don't get just a little bit cross when I encounter stupidity. It outrages me for God's sake. Mr. Plato's *Republic* . . . "not a very good story"!
BOBA: Do you think it is?
OUPA *(A pause and then reluctantly)*: No. I admit that as stories go it is bloody silly. But in any case, it's not a story the same as the ones I used to tell to you when you were small. It's an allegory, a metaphor, Boba. You mustn't take it at face value. It's got a hidden meaning and in this case it's about the nature of what we call the "real world." In any case, what I shared with you was a nutshell version of it. If you really want to know what it means you can take the book and read it at home. I don't need it anymore.
BOBA *(Backing away from the offered book)*: No thanks, Oupa.

OUPA: It does however deserve a measure of respect.

(Handling the book.)

This happens to be one of the "cornerstones of Western philosophy". . . or so the wise philosophers tell me. Not that that helps me very much.

(Boba notices that the old man is massaging his right hand with his left. Without saying anything, Boba takes the old man's right hand and starts to massage it, a natural part of their routine.)

No, Boba, when it comes to that little shadow there on the wall, I realize now that there was another lesson, a more important one that I could have learnt from you as I watched you there at your mother's feet trying to pick up a scrap of shadow . . . trying so hard to hold it, and play with it.

BOBA: I didn't know yet that shadows aren't real, Oupa.

OUPA *(A sad little shake of his head)*: Oh, Boba! It's already happened to you. But of course, shadows aren't real. We all know that . . . not so?

BOBA: That is what Mr. Plato said . . . isn't it?

OUPA: Yes . . . that is what he said. That is what we all say . . . shadows aren't real. Mr. Plato would have seen in that little baby crawling around on the floor an illustration of ignorance. Because he didn't yet know what is real and what is not real. But, you see, there was a man two thousand years later who didn't think like that. He would have looked at you in a different way to "Mr. Plato" and you and me . . . and everybody else. He wouldn't have seen you as just a silly little child who didn't yet know better. He would have seen you as someone who maybe

knew something that Mr. Plato and you and me had forgotten as we got older and "wiser." That man knew . . .
that you could see a world in a grain of sand and Heaven
in a wildflower, he believed that you could hold infinity in
the palm of your hand and eternity in an hour . . .

BOBA: I don't understand, Oupa.

OUPA: Of course you don't. And neither did I. Because you are
losing, and I already have, the innocence we are all born
with. Yes, believe it or not, but this grumpy old pisspot
was once also crawling around on the floor at his mother's
feet, trying to catch shadows and eat them.

(Pause.)

I sit here, Boba, waiting for the shadow of that hummingbird because I want to do that again. I want to hold it in
my hand.

BOBA: But, Oupa! . . .

OUPA: What?

BOBA: You can't.

OUPA: No?

BOBA: Do you think you can?

OUPA *(A little laugh)*: Yes! Maybe there is still more than just
a little bit of innocence left in you! Tell me, Boba . . . Can
you remember when you first held an orange in your little
hands? Or an egg? When you first saw the moon? When you
first saw a bird fly? When you first saw your own shadow?
Can you? Can you remember any of those momentous
moments in your life? It's a real question, Boba.

BOBA: No, I don't think I can, Oupa.

OUPA: Neither can I. But wouldn't you want to? I would.
I would give all the time I had left for just one day of
that innocence, one day of seeing the world as I did when
I first opened my eyes . . . You see, Boba . . . I wasted

my chances. I allowed the mystery and splendor to slip away through my fingers because I took it all for granted. So here I am now asking myself, Is it too late now for anything other than a dream? That same man who saw the world in a grain of sand and held infinity in his palm also said:

He who mocks the infant's faith
Shall be mocked in age and death.
He who shall teach the child to doubt
The rotting grave shall ne'er get out.

Instead of going down on my hands and knees and helping you catch that little shadow on the floor, I smiled at your innocent folly and looked forward to the time when you would be big enough to understand me when I explained to you that shadows aren't real things, that a grain of sand is just a grain of sand, and that a wildflower has got a nice long Latin name, and that is the end of it. And that goes for the hummingbird as well. When I learned its so-called "real name"—its Latin name— I believed I knew something very important about it . . . Family: *Trochilidae*; Genus: *Calypte*; Species: *Anna*. *(Phony superior tone)* That is so much more impressive, don't you think, than just calling it that "precious little jewel of the garden." *(Shaking his head)* Oh, Boba . . . it's so so sad. I finally ended up thinking that the Latin name of a little daisy was a terribly important piece of information. And, year by year, my world became general; it lost its wonderful specificity. There were of course still moments when I broke through that crust of pseudo-knowledge and saw things with the eyes of that little toddler trying to catch his piece of shadow. *(Laughing with his recollection of a moment in his past)*

BOBA: You saw a hummingbird, Oupa?

OUPA: No. This was long before I came to this country and saw my first hummingbird.

BOBA: Are there no hummingbirds in Africa?

OUPA: No . . . we have what are called sunbirds. They can't fly backwards like the hummingbirds, but they are just as beautiful, and they also have long beaks and sip nectar from the flowers. One of their favorite flowers is that of the aloe plant, and in my home back there I had a thick hedge of them on the side of the house. Every spring that thorny impenetrable hedge would push up a miniature forest of red blooms. *(Laughing)* My God, it was beautiful, Boba! And there was one morning, one wonderful spring morning I will never forget—five of them—five sunbirds flying around in that forest of flowers! I counted them—male and female Malachite, and three Double-collared Sunbirds—and all their colors: green, ruby red, yellow, sparkling in the sunlight as they hopped from flower to flower dipping their beaks in. And standing there admiring them, ravished by the perfection of that moment was me, a young man with vigor and strength in his body. We were all part of it. That moment wasn't about a specimen of Homo sapiens admiring specimens: *Nectarina Famosa* and *Nectarina Chalybea* pollinating Aloe arborescens. It was about me . . . ME! . . . and five of God's jewels celebrating all of the created world and me shouting hallelujah . . . Yes, Boba, I did shout it . . . but ever so softly because I didn't want to break the spell of that moment. That young man had somehow managed to hang on to something of the magic he had as a small child . . . but with time . . . *(A despairing gesture)* . . . look at me now! There is no mystery or magic in the world I live in now . . . the so-called "real" world, and I am sick of it. I don't know how much time I've got left, Boba, but whatever there is, I just want once more to catch shadows and taste them. There's a nice Latin name for that as well—senile dementia—that's what they'll call it and then your dad will lock me away somewhere safe, but I don't give a damn. I'm sick of my rational existence in the "real world." I want to live once again in one full of mystery and magic and shadows I can play with.

BOBA *(Pointing to the wall)*: So are you going to catch that shadow, Oupa?

OUPA: Yes.

BOBA: When?

OUPA: When I can believe it's real. Yes. It's not a game of make-believe, Boba. I've got to really believe that that strange little intruder that flies around there on the wall every morning is as real as this old arthritic hand. Only then will I want to reach out and try to catch it.

BOBA: But you won't, Oupa.

OUPA *(Laughing)*: But I won't know that, Boba! Don't you understand. I won't know any of your sensible reasons for knowing that I would be wasting my time. You can join all the others in saying, "Poor old Oupa he's . . ." what's the phrase, Boba . . . "he's lost it, lost the plot, lost his marbles." But I won't give a damn. I'll be too busy catching shadows.

(He has allowed himself to get too excited. Another spell of short breath and chest pains. A frightened Boba goes to his side as he collapses in his chair.)

I'm all right . . . I'm all right! Glass of water . . .

(Boba fetches the glass of water and hands it to Oupa, who takes it and drinks, then strokes Boba's head.)

BOBA: Can I join in when you do it?

OUPA: Yes, of course. I will welcome any help I can get. But remember . . . it will be mine when we do catch it.

BOBA: Okay, but what will happen to it when you die?

OUPA: I'll leave it to you in my will.

BOBA: You will?

OUPA: Yes I will, in my will.

BOBA: Thank you, Oupa. I gotta go now. Will you be all right?

OUPA: Yes. When will I see you again?

BOBA: I'll come tomorrow.

OUPA: Promise?

BOBA: I promise. But I won't be able to stay as long as today.

OUPA: I understand. But please do come—even if it's just to say hello and good-bye.

BOBA *(Pausing at the door, looking at the wall)*: Please don't catch it today, Oupa. Wait until I'm with you.

OUPA: Promise.

(Boba leaves.

Oupa remains seated in his chair for a few seconds, then gets up and hobbles over to the door.)

Boba! Boba!

BOBA *(Offstage)*: Yes, Oupa?

OUPA: Tomorrow?

BOBA: Yes, Oupa. I promise.

OUPA: Be careful when you cross the road!

(The old man moves to his desk, picks up a fountain pen and his current notebook, which is mostly empty. Speaking aloud as he writes:)

June 11, 2014
   Today, I . . .

(Leaving the notebook open, and with his pen still in his hand, he returns to his chair. He takes a thick book from the side table and starts to read. The sunlight on the wall begins to fade. After a few moments, and the turning of a page, he reads something and pauses. He stares into space for a few seconds, then goes back to the previous page and picks up his reading from the bottom of it. This time he reads very carefully aloud:)

As he fell asleep he had still been thinking of the subject that now always occupied his mind—about life and death, and chiefly about death. He felt himself nearer to it.

"Love"? What is "love"? he thought. Love hinders death. Love is life. All, everything that I understand, I understand only because I love. Everything is, everything exists, only because I love . . .

(He moves to his desk and puts the book down. Reciting from memory:)

All, everything that I understand, I understand only because I love. Love . . . love . . . everything . . .

(He resumes writing in his notebook, reading aloud as he goes:)

Today, I . . . thought again about life and death.

(Hunched over at the desk, he continues writing, this time without speaking aloud, as the light in the room fades.
It darkens into a deep blue midnight hour. A square of light appears slowly on the wall.
The old man raises his head and looks at the wall.)

A soft seductive humming—it could be that of a woman—fills the air as the shadow of the hummingbird flies into the square of light on the wall. The old man sees it. He stands up and slowly approaches it. When he is within touching distance, he reaches out an arthritic hand, but it evades his touch. He tries again and again, but each time the shadow skips away as the humming turns into a gentle, teasing laugh. It invites him to laugh as well, and he does.

The shadow now leaves the wall, and he chases it around the room, which slowly fills with all the living colors of the hummingbird. The two laughing voices become ecstatic, but then are abruptly silenced by another severe spasm of coughing and chest pains from the old man.

The colors in the room fade as he staggers to his chair and collapses in it. He sits there with his head lowered onto his chest.

The gloom in the room fades slowly into the light of a new day.

We see Boba standing at the door.)

BOBA: Oupa! Oupa!

(Pause . . . and then softly . . .)

Oupa?

(He puts down his backpack and goes to his grandfather.)

Oupa!

(He reaches out and takes the hand of the old man in his. After a second or two of massaging it, he stops. He drops the lifeless hand suddenly and backs away. He looks

around wildly, and, after one more look at his grandfa-
ther, picks up his backpack and runs out of the room.
The light fades on the old man in his armchair.
The shadow of the hummingbird flies on the wall.)

THE END

ATHOL FUGARD was born in 1932 in Middelburg, in the Karoo desert region of South Africa. He has written more than thirty plays, four books and several screenplays. His plays include *Blood Knot* (1961), *Boesman and Lena* (1969), *"Master Harold" . . . and the boys* (1982), *The Road to Mecca* (1984) and *My Children! My Africa!* (1989). Many of his works were turned into films: *Tsotsi*, based on his 1980 novel, won the 2005 Academy Award for best foreign language film. His work spans the period of apartheid in South Africa (imposed in 1948), through the first democratic elections (April 27, 1994), when Nelson Mandela became president, and into present-day post-apartheid South Africa. One of the most performed playwrights in the world, and South Africa's best-known playwright, at eighty-one, Fugard continues to direct and write plays. Although he still travels regularly, as of 2013, he regards his house in the Karoo village of Nieu Bethesda, South Africa, as his permanent home.

Born in 1985 South Africa to a family in the diplomatic service, PAULA FOURIE spent the majority of her childhood living in the U.S. and Europe, returning to South Africa without having witnessed firsthand the turbulent final years of apartheid. Having begun writing in her teenage years (also winning a national writing competition with a short story in 2002), she has continued her creative writing alongside her work as a musicologist and choral conductor. In 2013, she obtained her PhD from Stellenbosch University, with a biography of South African musician and musical theatre composer Taliep Petersen as her dissertation. Her published academic work includes book reviews, interviews and journal articles, and she is currently reworking her manuscript on Petersen for publication. Writing in both English and Afrikaans, her poetry has appeared in several South African poetry journals. Fourie has been working with Athol Fugard since 2012. This is her first published excursion into the world of playwriting.